I0426352

NAVMC 2795

USMC
User's Guide
to Counseling

United States Marine Corps

PCN 100 013485 00

DEPARTMENT OF THE NAVY
HEADQUARTERS UNITED STATES MARINE CORPS
WASHINGTON D C 20380 0001

IN REPLY REFER TO
NAVMC 2795
MMCE
21 Jul 86

FOREWORD

1. PURPOSE

NAVMC 2795, U.S. Marine Corps User's Guide to Counseling, provides a means to assist Marine leaders and their Marines to be continuously motivated toward more effective individual performance. As in all Marine Corps leadership programs, increased unit readiness is the goal.

2. INFORMATION

a. The use of this Guide does not replace time-tested techniques of leadership or demand adherence to new, theoretical management techniques. The Guide provides a tool that focuses on creating an ingrained counseling ethic as a part of the Marine Corps leadership program.

b. The Guide reemphasizes the teacher-scholar, father-son relationship envisioned by General Lejeune. By its own definition, this Guide establishes a more effective means of communication and understanding between senior and junior; it continually strives to improve Marine Corps readiness.

3. FREQUENCY

This Guide will be reviewed annually and revised as necessary.

4. RESPONSIBILITIES

All seniors have a responsibility to their junior Marines to provide them with effective counseling. The key to accomplish this responsibility is the development of sound counseling skills by unit leaders to teach and to guide junior Marines to become more productive. The principles outlined in this Guide are in conformance with this concept.

5. ACTION

a. Commanding officers/officers in charge shall present this Guide to their Marines when promoted to the grade of corporal.

b. Submit requisitions for quantities of up to 25 copies of this NAVMC to the Marine Corps publications stock point at Marine Corps Logistics Base, Albany, Georgia (Code 876). For quantities in excess of 25 copies, submit a letter of justification to the Commandant of the Marine Corps (HQSP-2).

6. RESERVE APPLICABILITY

This Guide is applicable to the Marine Corps Reserve.

7. CERTIFICATION

Reviewed and approved this date.

DISTRIBUTION: L1L
ACTDU/ACTRES CPL THRU GEN
7230009 (9000)
4175001 (2000)
7230028 (600)
7000045/125 (50)

Copy to: 8145001 (1)

LOCATOR SHEET

Subj: USER'S GUIDE TO COUNSELING

Location: _____
(Indicate location(s) of copy(ies) of this Guide.)

USER'S GUIDE TO COUNSELING

RECORD OF CHANGES

Log completed change action as indicated.

Change Number	Date of Change	Date Received	Date Entered	Signature of Person Entering Change

USER'S GUIDE TO COUNSELING

TABLE OF CONTENTS

CHAPTER 1

INTRODUCTION

CHAPTER 1

INTRODUCTION

1001. PURPOSE OF COUNSELING

1. Developing people to their highest potential is a basic
leadership responsibility. Counseling is one means of
accomplishing this. Counseling involves two-way communication
between a Marine senior and a Marine junior to help the junior
achieve or maintain the highest possible level of performance.

2. Counseling is done on a regular basis by the senior officer,
staff noncommissioned officer (SNCO), or noncommissioned officer
(NCO) to whom the junior reports. While the senior may give
direction, the junior must also take an active part in the counseling process. The role of the senior is to help the junior to
achieve or maintain desired levels of performance and to plan
ahead. The junior is responsible for meeting the objectives that
develop during the counseling process.

3. The counseling process involves supporting and reinforcing
good performance as well as correcting deficiencies. It is a
positive, forward-looking process that focuses on improving
performance.

4. Counseling helps to keep Marine leaders and their Marines
directed toward effective individual performance and, thus,
toward increased unit readiness and effectiveness.

1002. BACKGROUND OF THE U.S. MARINE CORPS COUNSELING PROGRAM

1. The U.S. Marine Corps Counseling Program originated in the
recommendations of a 1983 study of the Marine Corps Performance
Evaluation System directed by the Deputy Chief of Staff Manpower,
Headquarters Marine Corps. The study concluded that counseling
is equal in importance to performance evaluation and that it
should be established as a separate, complementary program and be
clearly distinguished from performance evaluation. This conclusion was based on the contention that performance evaluation
focuses on past performance, while counseling focuses on future
performance. The conclusion was reinforced by the comments of
Marine Corps general officers that deficiencies existed in
counseling and that additional emphasis was needed in this vital
area of leadership.

2. On 30 November 1983, the Commandant of the Marine Corps
directed the Commanding General of the Marine Corps Development
and Education Command to study counseling and to develop a
continuing education program for application down to and
including unit levels for the improvement of individual

performance through regular counseling. The Director of the
Marine Corps Command and Staff College formed a task group for
this purpose - to plan a Marine Corps-wide counseling program.
The task group submitted the report, USMC Performance Counseling
Program, in 1984. The group recommended the design of a
counseling program that would be compatible with traditional
Marine Corps mores and values. The report provided the basis for
the new Counseling Program explained in this Guide.

1003. MARINE CORPS POLICY ON COUNSELING

1. The MCO 1610.12 provides the policy for the Counseling
Program.

2. The Order establishes a number of objectives for the
Counseling Program as follows:

     a. To maintain counseling as an integral and continuous part
of traditional Marine Corps leadership.

     b. To develop counseling skills through a continuing
education program that teaches the importance of daily coaching
and provides the tools to conduct effective counseling.

     c. To increase individual performance and productivity
through counseling, and thereby increase unit readiness and
effectiveness.

     d. To enhance the leader's ability to improve the junior's
performance.

     e. Create the ethic of effective counseling in a climate of
solid leadership, and provide a system to enhance that ethic. By
so doing, the program will ensure that the leadership goals
captured in General Lejeune's words become reality:

     "...the relation between officers and enlisted men
     should in no sense be that of superior and inferior
     nor that of master and servant, but rather that of
     teacher and scholar. In fact, it should partake of
     the nature of the relation between father and son,...."

3. The Order states that counseling is a vital and essential
leadership tool for developing juniors, improving individual
performance, and enhancing unit productivity. It provides the
following:

     a. Every Marine will receive counseling; however, the format
and frequency will vary.

     b. Counseling will begin whenever a new senior/junior
relationship is established.

4. The Order indicates how the counseling process will proceed.

    a. Counseling for lance corporals and below will occur every 30 days.

    b. Counseling for corporals through colonels will begin with an initial counseling session approximately 30 days after the start of the senior/junior relationship. A follow-on session will occur approximately 90 days after the initial counseling session, and subsequent sessions will occur every 6 months (at a minimum) and more frequently, if necessary.

    c. All counseling sessions at all levels and for all grades will be conducted on an individual basis.

    d. It is recommended that some documentation of the counseling sessions will be kept.

5. According to the Order, action responsibility is assigned as follows:

    a. The Deputy Chief of Staff for Manpower (CMC(M)) shall have cognizance over policy and sponsorship of the program.

    b. The Deputy Chief of Staff for Training (CMC(T)) shall have cognizance over the counseling education programs conducted in the Marine Corps units and training institutions.

    c. Commanding officers shall ensure that maximum attention is given to counseling training in unit training programs for all officers, SNCO's, and NCO's. In addition, they shall ensure that counseling is conducted per the current edition of MCO 1610.12.

    d. All officers, SNCO's, and NCO's shall execute the provisions of this Guide in counseling their juniors.

1004. THE RELATIONSHIP OF COUNSELING TO PERFORMANCE EVALUATION

1. Performance evaluation is a formal process for the evaluation of an individual's past performance. It centers around the fitness report for sergeants and above and around proficiency and conduct marks for corporals and below. It provides part of the basis for official actions, such as promotions, duty assignments, etc.

2. Performance evaluation and counseling were formerly seen as part of the same process. The task group on performance evaluation and counseling, comments by general officers, and a number of independent studies all indicated that when counseling is tied to performance evaluation, the typical results are inflated evaluations and ineffective counseling.

3. While performance evaluation focuses on past performance,
counseling focuses on improving and maintaining future performance. Counseling should be a regular, continuing process.
Counseling may be conducted formally or informally. It may be
planned and scheduled, or it may occur as the need arises. To be
effective, however, it must be viewed as an integral part of the
day-to-day job of leadership. Counseling should be separate from
performance evaluation - although the two should be mutually
complementary.

4. It is important to distinguish performance counseling from
personal counseling. While personal counseling is also part of
the leader's responsibility, it focuses on helping an individual
Marine to solve personal problems. Such personal problems may
be addressed in the counseling process. The contents of the
counseling program must focus completely on the skills and
techniques of counseling, both personal and performance.

5. In short, counseling ties back to fitness reports - but only
as a basis for reinforcing or improving performance in the
future. Counseling may also include personal counseling - but
only as a means of influencing performance.

1005. OVERVIEW OF THE USER'S GUIDE

1. This Guide provides officers, SNCO's, and NCO's with an
introduction to the Marine Corps Counseling Program. It is a
continuing reference for use in planning and carrying out the
counseling process.

2. Chapter 2 gives an overview of the Counseling Program. It
describes the frequency of counseling, beginning with the initial
counseling session and including follow-on sessions and event-
related sessions. It reviews the counseling process; discusses
types of counseling; reviews the practices and skills of
counseling; and sets forth the benefits of counseling to the
senior, the junior, and the unit.

3. Chapter 3 covers the steps in the process of conducting a
counseling session - preparing for the session, opening the
session, conducting the session, closing the session, and
following up after the session has been completed.

4. Chapter 4 provides an in-depth review of counseling
practices - the skills involved in conducting effective
counseling. It includes the principal approaches to counseling - directive, nondirective, and collaborative. It also covers
the range of skills required to conduct an effective counseling
session - setting targets, problem solving, questioning, active
listening, giving feedback, and planning for improvement.

5. Chapter 5 identifies some of the most common problems that arise in the counseling process for both the senior and the junior. It presents ways of anticipating and dealing with them.

6. There are two appendixes to the Guide as follows:

    a. Counseling Worksheets

    b. Bibliography on Counseling

CHAPTER 2

OVERVIEW OF THE U.S. MARINE CORPS COUNSELING PROGRAM

CHAPTER 2

OVERVIEW OF THE MARINE CORPS COUNSELING PROGRAM

2001. FREQUENCY OF COUNSELING

1. The Initial Counseling Session (ICS)

a. The initial counseling session occurs whenever a new senior/junior relationship is established - that is, when a Marine first reports to a unit or when there is a change in the Marine's immediate supervisor. (The immediate supervisor is the next senior person who is directly responsible for the primary tasking and leadership of the junior Marine.) The initial counseling session does not replace the traditional "welcome aboard" meeting, which occurs immediately. The initial counseling session should occur approximately 30 days after the start of the senior/junior relationship. It must establish the junior's goals for the next few months as well as a common set of expectations about the junior's performance.

b. The initial counseling session should lay the groundwork for an effective, productive working relationship between the senior and the junior. It should be scheduled and planned (in advance) and should be designed to accomplish several objectives as follows:

(1) To make the senior's expectations clear.

(2) To ensure that the junior understands those expectations.

(3) To set goals or targets and make plans for the junior to meet those targets.

(4) To convey the senior's interest and concern.

(5) To help the junior understand the senior's leadership style.

(6) To motivate the junior to achieve the highest possible level of (future) performance.

(7) To ensure that the junior understands the mission and status of the unit and the junior's primary and collateral duties.

c. Both the senior and the junior should prepare for the initial counseling session. The agenda should provide for a review of the mission and status of the unit, the junior's duties in the unit, and the targets that should be set for the junior - both for the job at hand and for overall professional development.

2. Follow-On Sessions

    a. For corporals through colonels, a follow-on session
should be held approximately 90 days after the initial counseling
session, and subsequent sessions should be held at intervals of
no more than 6 months.

    b. The purpose of these follow-on sessions is to ensure that
the junior is on track. A follow-on session should deal with
both strengths and weaknesses. It should reinforce the junior's
successes and attempt to correct deficiencies. It should
identify and analyze any performance problems that have emerged
since the last counseling session, and it should focus on
identifying a mutually agreed-upon solution to those problems.
During the follow-on session, the senior and the junior should
review the junior's progress toward achievement of the targets
established at the last session and should modify them or add new
targets, as appropriate.

    c. The process involved in the follow-on session is
essentially the same as in the initial counseling session. Both
participants should prepare for the session, and it should follow
a predetermined agenda. Both parties should also participate
fully and actively. As the junior develops experience in the
unit, the junior can be expected to take a more active part in
the process.

3. Counseling for Lance Corporals and Below

    a. Lance corporals and below should receive counseling every
30 days to ensure current and frequent feedback. These Marines
will provide the Marine Corps with its future NCO and SNCO
leadership. Their Marine skills must be developed through a
conscientiously applied program and in an environment where
specific, detailed, and concrete guidance is given to achieve the
unit mission.

    b. Counseling for lance corporals and below should be
conducted by the immediate supervisor, who is normally an NCO.
NCO's are the first link in the chain of command. They work most
closely with lance corporals and below, issue them orders, and
supervise them on a daily basis. NCO's are in the best position
to judge actions, offer guidance, or recognize a good job.

    c. Lance corporals and below must know what is expected of
them and how they will be measured regarding those expectations.
This is especially important after boot camp, when young Marines
must begin to rely more heavily on their own initiative and
motivation. This challenge is easier when they are given
specific targets and standards for which to strive. It is
difficult to meet expectations of their seniors unless they know
what those expectations are.

d. The counseling sessions should be brief "blanket on the footlocker" or locker box-type sessions lasting approximately 10 to 15 minutes. The junior's strengths and weaknesses should be discussed, and guidance should be provided on how to improve.

e. This is also a time when a variety of other topics could be discussed. For example, these topics could include pay-related matters, the Marine's Leave and Earnings Statement (LES), the family, or furthering education through off-duty education or Marine Corps Institute (MCI) courses. This is also a time when personal goals can be discussed or when the senior may clarify upcoming events that could affect the junior's personal life.

f. An exception to the 30-day counseling period should be made for reservists. Reservists should be counseled every 3 months and once during annual training duty.

4. Interim Reviews and Event-Related Counseling Sessions

a. Counseling can occur at any time; it need not be limited to formal, scheduled follow-on sessions. It can be initiated by either party.

b. The senior should initiate a session of this kind as soon as possible when there is a need. It is important to remember that a counseling session can be an occasion for praise as well as for dealing with problems. Counseling should be a means of reinforcing a Marine's strengths as well as correcting deficiencies.

c. Meeting with the senior for a counseling session - however brief and informal it may be - keeps the junior aware of the senior's interest and concern. It also gives the senior and the junior an opportunity to deal with problems before they become serious.

5. Relationship to Performance Evaluation

a. Performance evaluation focuses on the past. Counseling also considers the past, but only as a means of directing attention to improving performance. The senior who counsels a junior may not be the same senior who does the performance evaluation.

b. The two processes are separate but complementary. The counseling process helps the senior to build a body of systematic observation of the junior's performance - based on well-defined targets and standards. As a result, the performance evaluation process should not produce any surprises for either party; and the evaluation is more likely to be balanced, comprehensive, and accurate than it would be if counseling had not taken place on a regular basis. By the same token, the periodic performance

evaluation can help to clarify and crystallize the subjects on
which the counseling process should focus.

2002. THE COUNSELING PROCESS

1. Formal Counseling. The counseling process is conducted in
formal, planned sessions and in informal, unscheduled, event-
related sessions. Formal counseling occurs at the initial
(counseling) session and during follow-on sessions. These
sessions should be scheduled and conducted according to an
agreed-upon agenda. During these sessions, the senior should
draw on the full range of counseling practices and skills. These
sessions usually focus on the junior's overall performance and on
targets over a period of several weeks or months.

2. Informal Counseling. As noted, informal counseling sessions
can occur at any time, and they can be initiated by either party.
Such a session typically occurs because either the senior or the
junior sees a need before the next scheduled follow-on session.
Informal sessions are likely to be short and usually focus on a
specific recent event. The senior may not have to draw on the
full array of counseling techniques, and any planning or target
setting that occurs is likely to focus on the short term.

2003. TYPES OF COUNSELING

1. Directive Counseling. With the directive approach, the
senior carries the ball, analyzing the situation, developing a
solution or a plan for improvement, and telling the junior what
to do. This approach is "senior centered." The senior is open
and frank about influencing the junior to be one kind of person
rather than another.

2. Nondirective Counseling. With the nondirective counseling
approach, the senior asks questions, listens, and draws the
junior out. The senior helps the junior to analyze the situation
and to develop the solution or plan for improvement. This
approach is "junior centered." The junior is encouraged to talk,
to be trouble free, and to have a clear mind while the senior
plays the role of a person willing to help - mostly by listening.
The goal of the nondirective approach is to help the junior
become more mature and to develop personal resources. The junior
"owns" the problem and the solution.

3. Collaborative Counseling. A third option, the collaborative
counseling approach, draws on both the directive and nondirective
techniques. It offers the senior greater flexibility. It
promotes joint diagnosis. The junior and the senior work as a
team to diagnose and solve the junior's problem. This approach
can succeed if the junior accepts the senior and is eager to

solve the problem. With the collaborative counseling approach, the senior may emphasize directive or nondirective approaches - depending on the subject of the discussion, the purpose in mind, and the sense of how well the discussion is going.

2004. COUNSELING PRACTICES

1. Practices Related to the Junior's Performance. Some counseling practices focus primarily on the nature of the performance that is expected of the junior. Such practices include the following:

    a. Target setting - defining what the junior will be expected to do as a result of the counseling session and setting the standards by which effectiveness will be judged.

    b. Problem solving - analyzing the junior's performance problems and developing solutions to them.

    c. Planning for improvement - developing a plan to build on the strengths of the junior or to overcome shortcomings.

2. Practices Related to the Senior's Counseling Activities. Some counseling practices are concerned with getting the most productive results from the counseling session. They may be used in target setting, problem solving, planning for improvement, or other aspects of the meeting. They include the following:

    a. Questioning - using a variety of questioning techniques to draw the junior out or to clarify what is said or thought.

    b. Giving feedback - letting the junior know what the senior thinks about performance or summarizing what the senior understands to be going on in the meeting.

    c. Active listening - interpreting what the junior is saying and observing what is being done (identifying verbal or nonverbal cues that indicate thoughts or feelings that may not be expressed directly).

2005. BENEFITS OF THE COUNSELING PROCESS

1. Counseling, if it is carried out well, benefits the senior, the junior, and the unit as a whole.

2. The senior benefits by knowing that the expectations are understood, that guidance has been provided toward meeting those expectations, and that there has been a significant contribution made to the development of the individual Marine - one of the most important responsibilities of the leader.

3. The junior benefits by knowing where the junior stands, what the senior thinks of the junior's performance - good or bad, and what must be done to reach full potential as a Marine.

4. The unit benefits when all of its members give continuous attention to the effectiveness of their performance and work to improve performance wherever it can be improved, thus increasing overall unit effectiveness and readiness.

CHAPTER 3

PLANNING AND CONDUCTING A COUNSELING SESSION

CHAPTER 3

PLANNING AND CONDUCTING A COUNSELING SESSION

3001. PREPARATION

1. The most effective counseling sessions have thorough advance preparation. Both the senior and the junior should prepare for the session. Figure 3-1 provides an overview of the counseling process.

2. Reviewing and Evaluating Performance

a. The first step in preparing for a counseling session is to review and to evaluate the junior's performance since the last session. The review should cover everything that was planned at the last counseling session and anything that has occurred in the meantime that either party thinks should be discussed. The review should be as detailed and specific as possible. It should cover both good and bad performance - performance that the senior (or the junior) considers praiseworthy as well as problems that need correction.

b. To ensure having a complete, balanced picture of the junior's performance for the period to be discussed, the senior should keep informal notes for reference when the time comes to prepare for the counseling session. The leader's notebook is the ideal place for such notes. The notes should serve as a memory-jogger to ensure that the senior does not forget or overlook events needing attention in a counseling session - particularly things that happened several weeks or months before the session.

3. Defining Objectives. Both the senior and the junior should have a clear idea of what they want to accomplish in the counseling session. To this end, they should identify the successes, failures, and problems that should be covered. This stage of the planning process should include the analysis of performance problems, development of some tentative solutions for them, and identification of the junior's targets for the next performance period.

4. Setting the Agenda

a. The agenda should reflect the objectives for the session. The topics to be covered should be in the sequence in which the senior would like to discuss them. For example, it is often desirable to start the session with positive comments on the performance that the senior wants to praise and reinforce. Save discussion of problems and difficult issues until both parties are warmed up and feeling comfortable.

Steps	Activities	Counseling Skills
1. Preparation	a. Review current performance. b. Determine what counseling is to accomplish. c. Have subordinate provide inputs. d. Determine how to conduct the meeting.	a. Setting targets. b. Problem solving.
2. Opening	a. State expectations for the meeting. b. Establish a good climate.	a. Questioning. b. Active listening.
3. Main Body		a. Setting targets. b. Questioning. c. Giving feedback. d. Active listening. e. Problem solving.
4. Closing	Plan for improvement.	Planning for improvement.
5. Follow-up	a. Make personal counseling notes of the meeting. b. Monitor performance. c. Continue the process. Plan new actions when current actions are achieved or completed.	a. Problem solving. b. Questioning. c. Giving feedback. d. Setting targets. e. Planning for improvement.

Figure 3-1.--AN OVERVIEW OF THE COUNSELING PROCESS

b. The senior should ask the junior for suggestions on the agenda, and they should agree on it for the session. The agenda should be written in advance - preferably in their notebooks.

c. The senior should also give some thought to the counseling approach that will be used during the session. Should it be primarily directive? Nondirective? A combination of both approaches? This decision will depend on the senior's assessment of the situation - the amount of time that the session should take, the junior's readiness to confront performance problems, and the seriousness of the problems.

d. The senior should give some thought to the questions that may be asked during the session. While the session need not and should not be "scripted" in advance, the senior may find it helpful to identify a few key questions on the most important issues for use in focusing the discussion.

5. Scheduling the Time and Place of the Session. The counseling session should be scheduled enough in advance so that both parties have sufficient time to prepare for it. The senior should ensure that the calendar is clear. There should not be any interruptions. Time should be set aside for the session so that everything on the agenda can be covered. Generally, formal sessions (an initial counseling or follow-on) will take from 45 minutes to an hour to complete.

6. The Setting for the Session

a. It is important that both parties be relaxed, talk comfortably and easily. It is important that full attention be given to the counseling session. It can be disconcerting or even a humiliating experience for a junior to talk to a senior who is only giving partial or sporadic attention. Anything other than well-focused attention can easily be interpreted as meaning that the problems and the junior as a person are unimportant.

b. You can increase your effectiveness and credibility when you "clear" your mind as much as possible before attempting to counsel someone. "Mind clearing" may include taking care of anything "urgent" or "pressing" that might interrupt your thought process once the session has started. It may be better to keep the junior waiting a few minutes so that you can say: "Thanks for waiting. I had to take care of some personal matters so that I could give you my full attention."

c. Sometimes, however, in spite on one's best effort to clear your mind, you may find some cue. perhaps even something that the junior says, that brings to mind an unresolved problem or forgotten task. Instead of trying to force your mind back to the task at hand, it may be helpful to simply say, for example: "Your mention of a driver's license reminds me that mine is about

to expire. Let me make a note of that so it won't become a
distraction, and we can continue our discussion."

     d. It has been demonstrated that even if one attempts to
disregard an internal disruption, there is a good chance that
one's face or posture will indicate that something is wrong. If
you choose to hide your thoughts or feelings, the other person
may be confused and incorrectly assume he/she is responsible for
your reaction. Some clues are as follows: a person's eyes begin
to focus behind or beside you, the breathing or skin color may
change, or the hands may begin to fidget, etc. If the senior
notes such occurrences, it may help to ease the junior if the
senior were to simply say, "I notice that you're tapping your
fingers, does that indicate that there is something else on your
mind that needs to be considered?"

     e. Outside disruptions can confuse and interrupt the flow of
an exchange to the point where rapport is lost and considerable
time must be spent recovering before the session can continue. A
little preplanning can prevent many disruptions that might
otherwise occur; for example, let others know that you will be
counseling and do not wish to be interrupted. If, however, you
are disrupted, handle it promptly and be as open as possible with
the junior.

     f. The comfort of each person needs to be considered.
Frequently, such matters as a nervous junior's need for fresh air
or the light into which the junior might be staring are overlooked. Give consideration to appropriate room temperature, and
avoid having either person face an unshaded window.

     g. The seating arrangement can also be important. For
example, facing each other across a desk may make the relationship too formal for relaxed discussion. The senior should
consider a seating arrangement that enhances the personal,
informal tone of the counseling process.

3002. OPENING THE SESSION. Two things are particularly
important in the opening moments of the session. First, a
climate should be established that is conducive to an open,
relaxed discussion. It is usually a good idea to begin with a
cup of coffee and a few minutes of small talk. Second, both
parties should understand why they are holding the session. To
ensure that they do, the senior should go over the objectives of
the session and the prepared agenda and should invite the
junior's comments before proceeding to the main body of the
session.

3003. CONDUCTING THE SESSION

1. Guiding the Discussion

a. While the counseling process must be a two-way interchange to be productive, the senior must guide the discussion to
ensure that all objectives set for the session are accomplished.
At the same time, the senior should be attentive and responsive
to the junior's reactions. For example, if the conversation
turns to Item C on the agenda before Item B has been covered, the
senior may choose to go ahead with Item C and come back to Item B
later.

b. The agenda should be a guide. While it should be
followed as closely as possible, the senior should also be flexible about it. The most important thing is to cover everything
fully and to move on when a subject has been fully discussed.

2. Encouraging the Junior's Participation

a. There are a number of counseling techniques at the
senior's disposal for promoting a two-way conversation and
keeping the junior actively involved. (These techniques are
discussed in detail in Chapter 4.) The senior should know these
techniques and develop skill in using them. They include various
kinds of questions and approaches for encouraging participation
by the junior.

b. In this process, the most important general rules for the
senior are to pay attention and to concentrate on what is heard
and seen during the session. Also, the senior must keep the
overall purpose of the counseling process in mind which is to
develop the junior's ability to evaluate performance clearly and
objectively and to take responsibility for improving performance,
thereby contributing to unit readiness.

3. Agreeing on Targets and Plans for Improvement

a. The last stage of the counseling session should define
the junior's targets and lay out plans for meeting them. Both
parties should enter the session with some idea of what these
targets should be. After all other items on the agenda have been
thoroughly aired, the senior should review earlier thoughts about
the targets, and the junior should do the same. The senior and
the junior may want to modify the targets - for example, make one
or more of the targets more challenging. They may want to add or
drop some. In any case, the senior must be satisfied that the
targets will accomplish what is considered most important in the
junior's future performance and overall development. The senior
must also ensure that the junior understands and agrees to the
targets.

b. Once the performance targets have been established, the junior should outline a plan for meeting them. The plan for improvement need not be elaborate, but it should be detailed and specific enough to satisfy the senior that the junior not only understands what is expected to be accomplished but has a clear idea of how to go about it.

3004. CLOSING THE SESSION

1. Before the session ends, the senior should take a few minutes to review and summarize the items discussed. The senior asks for the junior's comments to ensure that he/she understands the results of the session in the same way.

2. As the session ends, a few words of small talk may again be in order. The occasion is not a social one, but in many ways it is a highly personal one. It is especially important that the senior recognize this fact. It is especially important to end the session on a positive, encouraging, and forward-looking note.

3005. FOLLOW-ON

1. Documenting the Session

    a. The current edition of MCO 1610.12 recommends there should be some documentation of the counseling sessions kept. These would be along the lines of personal counseling notes.

    b. These notes would benefit both the leader and the Marine being led by serving as a quick reference in recalling the specifics of the counseling session between the junior and senior.

    c. It could just be an outline of the subjects discussed and guidance given. It would aid in ensuring the mutual understanding of responsibilities, expectations, and the direction of the junior.

    d. These notes would also serve as an aid so that during future sessions topics are not repeated unless required, and both junior and senior see the improvement in the objectives previously set.

    e. Essentially, the use of the small unit leader's/platoon commander's notebook is one method for recording the counseling notes.

    f. Appendix A provides sample worksheets for documentation. If the commander decides to use these forms, they can be modified as necessary to fit the unit's specific needs. The forms should

fit into the small unit leader's/platoon commander's notebook for
easy reference.

g. The two forms are organized in essentially the same way.
They provide space for recording three important aspects of the
session: the subject matter, the junior's targets or tasks for
the coming period, and notes on the junior's major accomplishments since the last counseling session, and/or comments on other
matters.

h. The worksheets can be filled in before the session to
help guide the discussion. After the session, both the senior
and the junior should make any necessary changes to reflect what
actually happened. Alternatively, the worksheets can be filled
in after the session. Whatever approach is used, it should be
the same for all of the counseling activities in the unit.

i. Documentation of a counseling session is for use only by
the senior and the junior. It is not to be forwarded to an
officer in the reporting chain, nor is it to be passed from one
senior to the next when the senior/junior relationship ends.
When the relationship is terminated, all documentation is
destroyed.

j. The counseling notes need not be elaborate or highly
formalized but should be specific and detailed enough to provide
at least the following information:

    (1) the date of the counseling session,

    (2) the name of the Marine who received the counseling,

    (3) the subjects that were discussed, and/or

    (4) the targets/tasks that were set.

2. Monitoring the Junior's Performance. The senior must pay
continuing attention to what happens after the counseling
session. From time to time, the senior should refer to the
performance targets agreed to at the session and make a judgment
as to how well the junior is meeting them. The senior should
continue to encourage and reinforce good performance and help the
junior correct deficiencies. In this process, the senior can use
the subjects of the counseling session and the targets that were
set as a framework for the continuing efforts to help the junior
improve and maintain a high level of performance.

USER'S GUIDE TO COUNSELING

CHAPTER 4

COUNSELING

CHAPTER 4

COUNSELING

4001. COUNSELING APPROACHES AND STYLES

1. Directive Counseling

a. In the directive approach, the senior takes the lead in
analyzing the junior's performance, identifying problems, and
laying out a plan for improvement. This is a senior-centered
approach with the junior playing a relatively passive role.

b. The military environment tends to influence the use of
the directive approach to counseling, and in some circumstances,
it can be the most productive approach. It takes less time than
the nondirective approach. For juniors who are immature, inexperienced, or unsure of themselves, it may be the only effective
form of counseling.

c. Directive counseling depends on an accurate diagnosis of
the junior's problem, which is often difficult. The senior has
to draw on information available from records, experience, and
knowledge of behavior. If the senior does not identify the
problem correctly or a workable solution, the senior could do
more harm than good.

d. Directive counseling has several potential drawbacks.
The most serious drawback is that it does not require the junior
to accept responsibility for the junior's actions. Directive
counseling puts the responsibility for success on the senior. By
attempting to direct the junior toward a solution of a problem,
the senior may become the "owner of the problem and the
solution." This may have an effect on whether the junior acts on
the advice given. Directive counseling is based on the notion
that a person with a problem needs information from someone else
to understand one's self.

e. Another limitation of the directive approach is the
possibility of focusing on the symptom rather than the cause and
the problem. The senior must determine the problem, define the
cause, and decide if others are involved or affected. If the
senior does not do this, the recommendation could cause
additional problems.

f. For these reasons, the directive approach should be used
sparingly. When it is used, it should not be confused with
giving an order. Directive counseling can be done with a combination of suggestion, explanation, persuasion, and demonstration
that helps the junior to become involved in the decision-making
process.

2. Nondirective Counseling

    a. In the nondirective approach, the senior asks questions,
listens, and uses a variety of techniques to draw the junior into
the discussion and reach personal decisions. This is a junior-
centered approach.

    b. Nondirective counseling takes more time than directive
counseling, and there is the risk of having rambling, incon-
clusive discussions. The senior must demonstrate a high degree
of counseling skill to achieve the results desired.

    c. The advantage of the nondirective approach is that it
requires the junior to think harder; to see personal performance
clearly and objectively; and to take responsibility for solving
personal problems, planning improvements, and making decisions.
When the nondirective approach is used skillfully, the advantages
outweigh the cost in time and effort.

3. Collaborative Counseling

    a. In practice, most counseling sessions involve a combi-
nation of the directive and nondirective approaches. Used
together, they can be more effective than when they are used
alone. The directive approach can be used to help focus a
rambling discussion. The nondirective approach can help to relax
tensions in an otherwise directive session.

    b. Combining the two approaches calls for special sensitivi-
ty on the part of the senior. The senior must be tuned in and
alert to the progress of the conversation so a shift from one
approach to another may be required depending on the situation.
The senior must understand the advantages and disadvantages of
each approach and must be able to move easily from one to the
other to keep the discussion moving forward in the most productive way possible.

4. Individual Counseling Styles

    a. Regardless of the approach that the senior uses, it must
not be an artificial technique applied self-consciously. One of
the fundamental rules of counseling is to be yourself. If the
senior behaves in a way that makes one personally uncomfortable,
the senior may appear to be insincere and perhaps manipulative.

    b. It is possible to learn counseling skills, just as it is
possible to learn to pitch a baseball or to fire a rifle.
Practice makes these skills come more easily. The senior should
accept the idea that counseling is a skill and should work at
developing it. Counseling skills should be incorporated into the
senior's leadership style; they should not cause a change in
style.

c. Regardless of the approach the senior is using and whether the purpose is for praise or for criticism, it is important to focus on performance and not on the person. Saying "That didn't work out" is better than saying "You couldn't make it work." Discussion of performance - particularly poor performance - can stir up strong emotions. The senior's tone, attitude, and the specific words used should be carefully chosen to minimize the junior's feeling of being judged rather than helped.

d. Being as specific as possible also helps to reduce the potential emotional charge of a counseling session. To say "Your company isn't measuring up" is a broad, sweeping, and general statement. To say "Your company took longer than it should have to get across that bridge" focuses the conversation on specific facts and events. It also makes it much easier for both the senior and the junior to find the cause of the problem, to agree on what it is, and to work out a solution together without having injured feelings get in the way.

4002. COUNSELING PRACTICES RELATED TO THE JUNIOR'S PERFORMANCE

1. Setting Targets

a. One of the most important objectives of a counseling session is to establish a set of targets for the junior to accomplish after the session is over. In many sessions, this will be the primary objective. Defining targets is a skill in its own right. If it is done well or badly strongly influences whether the junior's performance improves.

b. The target is to be achieved by the junior. It may be to keep performance at the current level. It may be to change it for the better. In either case, the target should be the object - not a process. For example, the target should not be "To work on improving the platoon's readiness," but "To achieve a 95 percent MCI completion rate by 31 December."

c. One difference between these two targets is clarity. The first target could mean almost anything from getting more equipment to increasing the intensity of the training program. There should be no question about what the second target means. It says exactly what kind of activity is involved - not just improving but reaching a specific completion rate.

d. A second difference is precision. The first target says nothing about how either the senior or the junior will know when it has been accomplished. The second target specifies a minimum numerical rate and a date. The second target is measurable; the first one is not.

   e. Not all performance targets can be stated in quantitative
or numerical terms. If this cannot be done, the targets can be
expressed in a way that indicates whether something has happened.
In other words, the targets can be observable even if they are
not measurable. For example, "To have individual equipment in
combat-ready condition" is not a quantitative target. Yet, both
the senior and the junior can tell whether the target has been
met.

   f. A well-defined target has certain characteristics. One
characteristic is the presence of an action verb - for example,
"to start," "to complete," "to pass," etc. Another characteristic is definition of the object of the verb - for example, "to
start training," "to complete personnel records," "to pass
tests," and so on.

   g. The third characteristic of a well-defined target is that
it includes one or more standards by which the observer can tell
whether it has been achieved. The standards may be quantitative - for example, "95," "by 15 October;" - or qualitative -
for example, "in combat-ready condition." In either case, both
the senior and the junior must know what the standards mean and
understand them in the same way. They can agree on whether the
standards (and hence the target) have been met. If the standards
have not been met, they can tell by how much and in what way the
junior has fallen short.

   h. In short, a target describes an action to be taken or a
goal to be achieved, and it indicates how to tell whether it has
been accomplished (the standard). Standards may be stated in the
following terms:

      (1) Quantity - how much?

      (2) Quality - how well?

      (3) Timeliness - when is it to be done or how long will
it take?

      (4) Manner - in what way is it to be done ("safely" or
"promptly," for example)?

   i. In addition to these methods of defining targets to
ensure that they are clear, the senior should keep some general
guidelines for effective target setting in mind.

      (1) The targets should be challenging but attainable.
They should make the junior stretch to bring out the junior's
best, but they should not be so challenging as to be impossible.

      (2) The junior should have the authority and resources
that are needed to achieve the targets.

(3) The targets should be important. They should be related to the unit's mission, and they should represent a significant part of the junior's duties.

(4) The targets should be limited in number. Seniors sometimes tend to write down all targets they can think of, and they end up with a list that could take years to accomplish. The senior should pick a few important targets - generally three to five - that will make a significant contribution to the junior's effectiveness and that can be accomplished before the next counseling session.

(5) The junior should participate in the target-setting process. The targets are personal, and the junior should have a sense of "ownership." The senior should determine the targets but should also encourage the junior to come up with individual targets. As far as possible, the target-setting process should be a joint effort.

(6) Targets should not be viewed as fixed and final for all times. Circumstances change. After the counseling session, if a target suddenly becomes unattainable for reasons that are beyond the junior's control, the target should be dropped or revised to reflect the new circumstances.

2. Problem Solving

a. Much of the counseling process involves finding ways to help the junior to improve performance - to identify and solve problems that limit effectiveness. The senior's job in this regard is to help the junior to identify each problem, its cause, and its solution.

b. Like target setting, the problem-solving process should involve both the senior and the junior. The more the junior contributes to the solution, the more effective it is likely to be. At the same time, the senior can usually draw on a broader background of knowledge and experience and can apply it while using a systematic approach to the problem-solving process.

c. One approach to this process uses three questions as the framework for analyzing a problem and for working out an effective solution. These questions are as follows:

(1) What is the problem?

(2) Is the junior part of the problem?

(3) Is the senior part of the problem?

d. To answer the first question - What is the problem? - the senior must compare actual and desired performance - for example,

the difference between the target and the accomplishment. The
senior should ask the following:

    (1) What is happening that shouldn't happen?

    (2) What is not happening that should happen?

    (3) What is happening that is off target?

Answering these questions will help to bring the nature of the
problem into clear focus.

    e. To answer the second question - Is the junior part of the
problem? - the senior must find out whether there is something
about the junior that is preventing effective performance. The
following series of questions can help to pinpoint the cause of
the problem:

    (1) Does the junior have the physical and mental ability
to perform up to expectations?

    (2) Does the junior know that performance is not meeting
expectations?

    (3) Does the junior know how the job is to be done?

    (4) Does the junior have the skills necessary to do the
job?

    (5) Is the junior's attitude getting in the way of
effective performance?

Answering these questions will help to sort out the underlying
causes of the problem.

    f. Finally, to answer the third question - Is the senior
part of the problem? - the senior must clarify the problem
further and help to focus attention on ways of solving it. A
series of questions can help to define the issues that should be
addressed in working out an effective solution. These questions
deal with aspects of the problem that may be outside the junior's
control such as the following:

    (1) Has the senior made the junior's targets clear? Is
there any confusion or uncertainty about what the senior expects
to be accomplished?

    (2) Has the senior failed to praise the junior when
performance has been up to expectations?

(3) Has the senior overlooked or failed to correct situations in which the junior did not perform up to expectations?

(4) Is the senior (or are others) making conflicting or competing demands on the junior's time?

(5) Is the junior unaware of or making inefficient use of time, people, equipment, or other resources that are available to get the job done?

(6) Does the junior have the authority and resources necessary to do the job?

g. Working through this series of questions and related sub-questions can help to lay the groundwork for a solution to the problem. The senior can identify problems that only the junior can do something about, those that only the senior can do something about, and those that they will have to work on together.

h. Once the problem is clearly understood, solutions can be developed. For example, problems that are traceable to the junior can be assessed to determine whether they are caused by deficiencies in knowledge, skill, or attitude.

i. A knowledge-related problem means that the junior does not know what to do or how to do it. A solution to this kind of problem must be to give the junior the information required. Appropriate corrective actions could include the following:

(1) Explaining or providing written material that defines what is supposed to be done and how it is to be done.

(2) Giving the junior training.

(3) Showing the junior how to do it.

(4) Giving the junior on-the-job direction or coaching.

(5) Giving the junior feedback on individual performance - when and how it is satisfactory or unsatisfactory.

j. A skill-related problem involves the junior's ability to coordinate eye, mind, and body in the performance of a task - whether it is firing a rifle or teaching a class. Corrective actions for a skill-related problem must provide the junior with opportunities for practicing the task itself. They might include the following:

(1) Observing the junior performing the task and then telling how well it was done or how it might be done better.

(2) Showing the junior what to do and how to do it.

(3) Giving the junior an opportunity to practice the task.

k. An attitude-related problem may involve the junior's feelings toward the billet, toward others in the unit, or toward the individual. Any solution to an attitude problem must be carefully planned to shape and guide the junior's feelings and thinking. Corrective actions must involve the junior in recognizing the problem and cooperating in its solution. They may include the following:

(1) Discussing the problem with the junior to identify the causes.

(2) Telling the junior your perception of the problem and what should be done about it.

l. Attitude problems may be easy to solve, or they may be virtually impossible to solve. No hard-and-fast rules can be offered. The senior must try to understand the causes of the problem and to find a corresponding solution.

m. Once a solution or a number of alternative solutions have been identified, the senior should test the solution(s) by asking questions such as the following:

(1) What is most likely to happen if this action is taken? Will it solve the problem, or will it create new and larger problems?

(2) Can the action be accomplished? Will it be appropriate for the situation?

(3) What will the action cost in terms of time, money, and morale?

(4) What are the likely benefits of the action? Is it worth doing?

(5) Will the senior be able to provide the necessary support and follow-through?

(6) Is this the simplest solution to this particular problem? Is there a simpler way?

3. Planning for Improvement

a. Once the junior's targets have been established and solutions to any problems have been identified, the junior should

work out plans for achieving the targets and overcoming the
problems. Like the other steps in the counseling process, this
should be a joint effort. If possible, the resulting plan should
be primarily the junior's plan.

   b. The plan for improvement need not be elaborate, but it
should be detailed and specific enough to satisfy the senior that
the junior understands what is required and that the junior has a
realistic idea about how to do it. The plan also gives both
parties a framework for tracking progress and for identifying
problems before they become serious.

   c. The plan for improvement should outline steps along the
way to achieve the targets or to solve the problems. For the
most part, it will involve actions by the junior; but if anyone
else will share any part of the responsibility, that fact should
be noted. It may also be appropriate to indicate the schedule
for carrying out the plan in terms of milestones and dates - to
the extent that this is practical, realistic, and useful.

4003. COUNSELING PRACTICES RELATED TO THE SENIOR'S COUNSELING
        ACTIVITIES

1. Questioning

   a. Questions are the most used and sometimes the most
effective of the counseling practices. The senior should be
familiar with the broad array of questioning techniques and the
results that they may yield.

   b. One way of looking at the subject is in terms of "closed-
end" and "open-end" questions. A good example of a closed-end
question is one that can only be answered by a "yes" or a "no."
"Did you take the test?" is an example. By itself, such a
question leads no further. It may point the way to another
question. For example, if the answer is "yes," the next question
might be "Did you pass?" - another closed-end question.

   c. In contrast, an open-end follow-up question might be "How
was it?" This kind of question invites or even compels the
junior to start talking and to begin revealing personal thoughts
and feelings.

   d. Both kinds of questions have their uses. On the whole,
during counseling sessions, closed-end questions should be used
sparingly because they do not encourage much participation from
the junior. With such questions, the burden is almost entirely
on the senior to keep the conversation alive and productive.

   e. Questions that begin with "who," "what," or "when," can
be closed-end questions. They can be useful in getting out the

facts, but they begin to create the atmosphere of a cross-examination if they dominate the discussion.

f. Open-end questions can be used to invite a free response from the junior without revealing the senior's point of view - for example, "How is the work going?" or "Why do you think that approach didn't work?"

g. Echo questions repeat a word or phrase the junior has used and can encourage further explanation - for example, "You got no response?"

h. Probing questions can be used to get additional information - for example, "Why do you think that happened?"

i. Interpretive questions can be used to clarify or amplify what the junior has said - for example, "Does that mean that you'll have to start over again?"

j. Confirming questions can be used to gain commitment - for example, "So, your platoon is now ready?"

k. This list of questions does not exhaust the possibilities by any means. It should suggest two things, however, such as the following:

(1) The senior should develop an awareness of the kinds of questions that may be used in the course of a counseling session.

(2) The senior should consciously cultivate skill and versatility in adapting this style of questioning to the subject at hand, the purpose in mind, and the responsiveness and emotional state of the junior.

2. Active Listening

a. Listening can be a passive or an active process. "Active listening" involves not only hearing what the junior says but also interpreting what it means, observing what the junior does as well as what is said, and responding in appropriate ways.

b. Active listening serves at least two purposes. First, it gives the senior more to work with in responding to the junior's words. The senior can choose a style of questioning or decide how to guide the discussion more effectively than merely plodding item by item through the agenda. Second, it helps to show the junior that the senior is interested and concerned with what is going on in the discussion.

c. One aspect of active listening is picking up verbal cues that the junior may or may not realize are being given. The

junior's tone of voice may be higher or lower than usual or
unsteady. The junior may hesitate or stammer over certain words
or subjects. Words may be clear or mumbled. The junior may talk
in specifics or in generalities. Cues like these may indicate
problems that the junior is unaware of or does not want to talk
about but that the senior may want to address.

   d. Another aspect of active listening is picking up non-
verbal cues. Again, the junior may not be aware of them, but
they can indicate an attitude or emotional state that does not
come through in the junior's words. For example, the junior may
avoid the senior's eyes or slump in the chair or sit unnaturally
erect. The junior may scowl or smile or may have clenched fists.
The senior should not attempt to be an amateur psychologist, but
should be sensitive to the signals that the junior is sending in
this way and should guide the discussion accordingly.

   e. Active listening includes "playing back" what you hear to
ensure that you understand what the junior means and to show that
you are interested in what the junior says.

   f. One way of doing this is to restate it - for example,
"You're saying that you find it difficult to work with that
person."

   g. Another way is to paraphrase what the junior said - for
example, "So, working with that Marine is turning out to be
harder than you expected."

   h. Still another way is to offer supportive statements that
recognize the validity of the junior's views or feelings without
necessarily indicating agreement - for example, "I can understand
why you might have thought that."

3. Giving Feedback

   a. To be effective, the junior needs to know where he/she
stands. The senior should make a regular effort to express an
opinion regarding the junior's performance. This feedback can
occur in a formal counseling session, or informal session, or
during casual encounters in the course of the day's work.

   b. Feedback on the junior's performance should be specific.
It should focus on particular events and actions, specifically as
follows:

      (1) It should be objective. It should focus on perfor-
mance - not the person or the personality.

(2) It should be balanced, touching on strengths and successes as well as problems and weaknesses. Praise is a powerful motivator, and it should be used at every opportunity.

(3) It should be related to the junior's targets. It should help to keep the junior's attention focused on the priorities of the unit as well as on personal priorities.

(4) It should be timely. The feedback should come as close to the event as possible - while it is still fresh in one's memory. For scheduled counseling sessions that cover an extended period, the senior should provide an overall review of the junior's performance but should include enough specific examples to make it clear.

4004. COUNSELING PRACTICES AND COUNSELING SESSIONS. Some counseling practices are more effective at the initial counseling session, and some are more appropriate for follow-on sessions. Some may be most beneficial at the beginning or the end of a counseling session and some in the main body. Figure 4-1 suggests the nature of this relationship as a framework for planning a scheduled counseling session.

Initial Counseling Session	Event-Related Session	Follow-On Session
Setting Performance Targets	Giving Feedback	Setting Performance Targets
Questioning	Problem Solving	Problem Solving
Active Listening	Planning for Improvement	Planning for Improvement

Figure 4-1.--PRIMARY COUNSELING TECHNIQUES USED BY TYPE OF SESSION

CHAPTER 5

AVOIDING PITFALLS IN COUNSELING

CHAPTER 5

AVOIDING PITFALLS IN COUNSELING

5001. THE JUNIOR'S BEHAVIOR

1. The problems that can arise in the course of the counseling process are as varied as the people who are involved in the process. Problems are more likely to occur in the early stages of a senior/junior relationship and with a young, inexperienced Marine. They may turn up, however, at any time.

2. Getting the junior to participate in the process in a meaningful way can be difficult - particularly at the beginning of the senior/junior relationship. At this point, the basic need is to build the junior's confidence so that the counseling process is not threatening. The senior should do everything possible to demonstrate approachability, interest, and ways to help the junior do a good job.

3. Signs of nervousness are usually obvious. The senior can respond to them directly - for example, by telling the junior to relax - or indirectly - by providing a relaxed atmosphere, by looking interested but not threatening, and by beginning the counseling session with praise.

4. While not obviously nervous, the junior will sometimes agree, without comment, to everything the senior says. This may mean that the junior is afraid to expose personal thoughts and feelings. It may mean that the junior would simply like to see the meeting conclude. In any case, the senior can deal with this situation by using open-end questions that compel an answer of more than one or two words and that invite an expression of opinion. The senior should not look for agreement for its own sake - although agreement on targets is an objective of the meeting; rather, the senior should look for an open interchange based on mutual respect and confidence.

5. The junior may disagree with the senior - for example, in the interpretation or evaluation of individual performance. This is not in itself a problem. In fact, in some cases, the junior may be right. The senior should lead a joint exploration of the subject using questioning and active listening to ensure that the issues are thoroughly understood and that the senior and the junior come to an agreement, if possible.

6. Occasionally, the junior may argue persistently, denying, and rebutting what the senior says. In such a situation, the senior should try to separate the emotion from the content of the discussion. While the junior may be right, the emotional tension will get in the way of a productive discussion. The senior

should stay calm and try to keep the conversation focused on
specific events and objective facts.

7.   The junior may try to shift the blame for deficiencies in
performance. Again, the first recourse is to get the facts out
and to agree on what they mean, if possible. Beyond that, the
senior may want to follow-up on the issue after the counseling
meeting with others in the unit. The immediate concern, however,
must be to get the junior to accept responsibility for personal
decisions and performance.

8.   The junior may be discouraged and depressed. In this situation, the senior should try to raise the junior's spirits
through praise or to help the junior see personal performance in
a more constructive light.

5002.   THE SENIOR'S BEHAVIOR

1.   Just as the senior's failings can have a negative impact on
the junior's performance, the senior can cause problems during
the counseling process.

2.   The first concern should be whether planning for the counseling session has been adequate. Things that may seem trivial -
like the lighting or temperature of the room - can have unexpect-
ed effects on a conversation about the performance of one of the
participants. The senior must give serious thought to the
details of the setting as well as to the content of the counseling session.

3.   Before and during a counseling session, the senior should be
aware of aspects of individual behavior that can interfere with
the productivity of the session. One fairly common problem, the
so-called "halo effect," develops when the senior draws conclu-
sions about all aspects of the junior's performance from one
event or even from one personal characteristic. This is one form
of inflexible behavior as the senior sees everything about the
junior through a single lens.

4.   Other elements of the senior's mindset may also be a factor
- for example, a personal bias or a stereotyped view of women,
enlisted personnel, Southerners, or whatever. The senior must
deal with people who are different in various ways. The senior
must take them all as they are; respect them for what they are;
and make a constant effort to focus attention on facts, events,
and targets and results.

5.   Apart from such personal characteristics, the senior can
cause trouble in the counseling session through failings in some
counseling skills. For example:

a. The senior may be inflexible in the counseling
approach - constantly taking the tough guy role, using only the
directive approach, rigidly following the sequence of subjects on
the agenda, and so on. The most effective counseling style is
flexible and adaptable to changes and to the behavior of the
junior.

b. The senior may do too much of the talking or interrupt
the junior to get personal views across. The junior must be
involved in the process, or the counseling will not result in
developing a sense of responsibility and commitment to a set of
goals.

c. The senior may not be attentive or responsive to what the
junior is saying and doing. Concentration is essential to effective counseling. The senior must pay constant attention not only
to the junior's words but also to the junior's emotional state.

d. The senior may use emotionally charged words that arouse
the junior's feelings - especially when the subject is a problem
with performance. On rare occasions, this may be necessary to
get the junior to respond; but, ordinarily, the senior should
make a conscious effort to keep the tone of the conversation
friendly and objective.

e. The senior may jump to a conclusion. The senior should
ensure that there are sound reasons for making any generaliza-
tions about the junior's performance or behavior.

f. The senior may talk too much in general terms. Since
generalities are open to differing interpretations, the senior
should focus as much of the conversation as possible on facts and
events.

g. The senior may be vague about the junior's performance
targets or the plans for achieving them. The senior should take
pains before the counseling session to define the targets clearly
and precisely.

h. Finally, the senior may not follow up effectively after
the meeting. The senior should document the counseling session
according to the unit's procedures and, above all, monitor the
junior's performance after the session. This ensures that the
junior is aware of the senior's continuing interest.

APPENDIX A

COUNSELING WORKSHEETS

1. Documentation of counseling is recommended, but specific procedures are up to the individual unit commanders. The worksheets provided here are suggested, not mandatory (see Figures A-1 and A-2). It is suggested, however, that some form of documentation be established. The documentation should at least include the following:

a. The date of the counseling session.

b. The name of the Marine who received the counseling.

c. The subjects that were discussed.

d. The targets/tasks that were set.

2. It is important to remember that documentation should provide information to which both the senior and the junior can refer to verify their understanding of a past counseling session and to help them in planning for the next one.

Name:_____ SSN:_____ Date:_____

Grade:_____ MOS:_____ Billet:_____

Subjects on Which Guidance Was Provided

_____

Tasks Assigned Next Period

_____

Major Accomplishments and/or Comments

_____

Marine Counseled   _____
Marine Performing Counseling _____
Target Date for Next Session _____

Figure A-1 -- COUNSELING WORKSHEET - LANCE CORPORAL AND BELOW

Name:_____   SSN:_____   Date:_____
                                                 ICS:_____
Grade:_____ MOS:_____ Billet:_____   Fol-on:_____

Agenda/Subjects Discussed

Targets for Coming Period and/or Comments

Major Accomplishments

Marine Counseled   _____
Marine Performing Counseling   _____
Target Date for Next Session   _____

Figure A-2 -- COUNSELING WORKSHEET - CORPORAL AND ABOVE

APPENDIX B

BIBLIOGRAPHY ON COUNSELING

Books

Albanese, Robert, Managing - Toward Accountability For Performance, 3rd edition (Homewood, IL, Dorsey Press, 1981).

Bennis, Warren and Manus, Burt, Leaders: The Strategies For Taking Charge (New York, Harper & Row, 1985).

Bernadin, H.J. and Beatty, R.W., Performance Appraisal: Assessing Human Behavior At Work (Boston, Kent Publishing Co., 1983).

Blanchard, Kenneth and Johnson, Spencer, The One Minute Manager (New York, William Morrow & Co., 1982).

Carroll, Stephen J. and Schneier, Craig E., Performance Appraisal And Review Systems (Glenville, IL, Scott, Foresman & Co., 1982).

Connellan, Thomas K., How To Improve Human Performance (New York, Harper & Row, 1978).

Deegan, A., Coaching: A Management Skill For Improving Individual Performance (Reading, MA, Addison-Wesley, 1979).

Drucker, Peter F., People and Performance (New York, Harper's College Press, 1977).

Fombrun, Charles J., Tichy, Noel M., and Devanna, Mary Anne, Strategic Human Resource Management (New York, John Wiley & Sons, 1984).

Fournies, F., Coaching For Improved Work Performance (New York, Van Nostrand Reinhold Co., 1978).

Gordon, Dr. Thomas., Leadership Effectiveness Training (Ridgefield, CT, Wyden Books, 1977)

Henderson, Richard I., Practical Guide To Performance Appraisal (Reston, VA, Reston Publishing Co., 1984).

Latham, G.P., and Wexley, K.N., Increasing Productivity Through Performance Appraisal (Reading, MA, Addison-Wesley, 1980).

Levy, Seymour, A Guide To Counseling: Developing Employees Through Performance Reviews (Larchmont, NY, Martin M. Bruce Publishers, 1976).

McGregor, Douglas M., Leadership And Motivation (Cambridge, MA, M.I.T. Press, 1966).

Maccoby, Michael, The Leader: A New Face For American Management (New York, Simon & Schuster, 1981).

Mager, Robert F., and Pipe, Peter, Analyzing Performance Problems: Or, You Really Oughta Wanna (Belmont, CA, Pitman Learning, Inc., 1970).

Mirenberg, Jesse S., Breaking Through To Each Other: Creative Persuasion On The Job And In The Home (New York, Harper & Row, 1976).

Peters, Thomas J., and Waterman, Robert H. Jr., In Search Of Excellence: Lessons From America's Best Run Companies (New York, Harper & Row, 1982).

Porter, Lyman W., Managerial Attitudes And Performance (Homewood, IL, Irwin, 1968).

Wylie, Peter, Problem Employees: How To Improve Their Performance (Belmont, CA, Pitman Learning, Inc., 1981).

Zalernik, Abraham, Human Dilemmas Of Leadership (New York, Harper & Row, 1966).

Zangwill, Willard I., Success With People: The Theory Z Approach To Mutual Achievement (Homewood, IL, Dow Jones-Irwin, 1976).

Zey, Michael G., The Mentor Connection (Homewood, IL, Dow Jones-Irwin, 1984).

Articles

Admire, LtCol John H., "Leadership and fraternization." Amphibious Warfare School: Advance Sheets and Annexes, pp. 168-171 (1984-1985).

Benson, LtCol J.H., "An Approach to performance counseling." Marine Corps Gazette, pp. 63-67 (January 1985).

Boucher, Norman, "In Search of Leadership." New Age, pp. 48-53 (October 1985).

Brache, Alan. "Seven prevailing myths about leadership." Training and Development Journal, pp. 120-126 (June 1983).

Cavanagh, Michael E., "Personalities at work." Personnel Journal, pp. 55-64 (March 1985).

Clawson, James G., "Interpersonal learning ladder." University of Virginia, Charlottesville, VA (1983).

Darter, Steven, "Save that job: transforming the poor performer." Research Management, pp. 23-26 (May/June 1985).

Earl, LtCol Robert L., "Two views on performance evaluation." Marine Corps Gazette, pp. 53-54 (October 1984).

Edson, Col J.J., "Counseling craze criticized." Marine Corps Gazette, pp. 32-33 (March 1985).

Holoviak, Steven J., and Holoviak, Sharon Brookens, "The benefits of in-house counseling." Personnel, pp. 53-59 (July/August 1984).

Lawrence, VAdm William P., "Common qualities of good leaders." Amphibious Warfare School: Advance Sheets and Annexes, pp. 47-48 (1984-1985).

Miles, J.B., "How to help troubled workers." Computer Decisions, pp. 66-76 (February 12, 1985).

Nette, Maj Kenneth A., "A philosophy of command." Amphibious Warfare School: Advance Sheets and Annexes, pp. 232-238 (1984-1985).

Orton, Ann, "Leadership: new thoughts on an old problem." Training, pp. 28-33 (June 1984).

Pressler, Jr., Eugene C. "Counseling the problem employee." Management World, pp. 41-42 (March 1981).

Scharfen, Col J.C., "Views on manpower." Marine Corps Gazette, pp. 52-57 (February 1985).

Schulze, MajGen Richard C., "Obedience, the unpopular military virtue." Amphibious Warfare School: Advance Sheets and Annexes, pp. 159-162 (1984-1985).

White, Robert N., "Corrective action: a treatment plan for problem performers." Personnel, pp. 7-9 (February 1985).

Wight, David T., "The split role in performance appraisal." Personnel Administrator, pp. 83-87 (May 1985).

Zey, Michael G., "Mentor programs: making the right moves." Personnel Journal, pp. 53-57 (February 1985).

www.ingramcontent.com/pod-product-compliance
Lightning Source LLC
Chambersburg PA
CBHW070819290526
45795CB00002B/767